Sports Great

STEPHON MARBURY

BASKETBALL

For Other *Sports Great Books* call:
(800) 398-2504

STEPHON MARBURY

Jeff Savage

—SPORTS GREAT BOOKS—

Enslow Publishers, Inc.

40 Industrial Road   PO Box 38
Box 398   Aldershot
Berkeley Heights, NJ 07922   Hants GU12 6BP
USA   UK

http://www.enslow.com

Library of Congress Cataloging-in-Publication Data

Savage, Jeff. 1961–
    Sports great Stephon Marbury / Jeff Savage.
        p. cm. — (Sports great books)
    Includes index.
    Summary: Profiles the life of the New Jersey Nets' Stephon Marbury including
his childhood, college days, and professional career.
    ISBN 0-7660-1265-4
    1. Marbury, Stephon, 1977– —Juvenile literature. 2. Basketball players—
United States—Biography—Juvenile literature. [1. Marbury, Stephon, 1977–
2. Basketball players. 3. Afro-Americans—Biography.] I. Title. II. Series.
GV884.M197 S28   2000
796.323'092—dc21
                                        99-050845

Printed in the United States of America

10 9 8 7 6 5 4 3 2 1

To Our Readers:
All Internet addresses in this book were active and appropriate when we went to press.
Any comments or suggestions can be sent by e-mail to Comments@enslow.com or to
the address on the back cover.

Illustration Credits: Andrew D. Bernstein/NBA Photos, p. 11; Andy
Hayt/NBA Photos, pp. 22, 26, 29; Barry Gossage/NBA Photos, pp. 31, 53; ©
Georgia Tech, pp. 34, 38, 40, 43; David Sherman/NBA Photos, p. 49; Jeff
Reinking, p. 20; Nathaniel S. Butler/NBA Photos, pp. 9, 45; Noren
Trotman/NBA Photos, pp. 14, 58, 60; Sam Forencich/NBA Photos, pp. 18, 51.

Cover Illustration: Noren Trotman/NBA Photos.

Contents

Chapter 1

A Homecoming

The Marburys had come to the game early. They filled the ninth and tenth rows behind the Nets bench at the Continental Airlines Arena in the Meadowlands for New Jersey's 1999 midseason game against the Dallas Mavericks. Stephon Marbury had just been traded to the Nets. His family was there to see his home debut in a Nets uniform. Stephon was so excited during his team's warm-up shoot-around that he kept sneaking peeks up at his family. Stephon's father sat wearing a dark blue Nets baseball cap and a proud smile. Stephon's four brothers stood chatting and laughing, and occasionally glancing down at the hardwood floor, happy for their brother, yet thinking maybe it could have been one of them wearing that Nets uniform. Uncles and aunts, cousins and friends, everyone was there except Stephon's mother, who had to stay home to nurse Stephon's ailing sister.

Stephon Marbury grew up in nearby Brooklyn and dreamed of someday playing professionally in the New York metropolitan area. He jumped for joy a week earlier when he learned that the Nets, so close to his hometown, had swung a deal to get him in a trade from the Minnesota Timberwolves. So did most Nets fans, who remembered Marbury just a few years earlier leading his high school to the New York state title. They knew Marbury was a winner, which was something the Nets were not. New Jersey had a disastrous 3–18 record entering that Mavericks game. It was no surprise that large sections of empty purple seats ringed the upper level of the arena. Still, the 14,976 fans who showed up cheered wildly when Marbury was the first Nets player to be introduced.

Marbury stands just six-feet two-inches tall. Normally, that height does not strike fear in the hearts of the towering players of the National Basketball Association. But Marbury's game is funky fresh, with a mixture of deft crossover dribbles, ankle-breaking moves, brilliant behind-the-back passes, and sticky defense. And Marbury hungrily lifts weights for a powerful upper body that has two benefits: the strength to win tug-of-wars for the ball, and a muscular canvas upon which to display his many tattoos.

On Marbury's right shoulder is the word "Prince," a nickname given to him by his brothers. Below that is his own nickname for himself; "Mr. Starbury." Farther down is a panther which Marbury says describes his game. "Panthers are very smart, cat-quick, so powerful, but they never harm other animals unless they have to eat—unless it's necessary," says Marbury. "They just do what they have to do to survive, and that symbolizes me." On top of Marbury's left arm is the phrase "Coney Island's Finest," referring to the neighborhood in Brooklyn where he grew up. Beneath that is an ink drawing of Marbury embracing his young daughter, Stephanie, with the words "Love of my life." And underneath his jersey is one more tattoo over his heart. It is the phrase "Two souls, 1 body," which is a tribute to his oldest brother, Eric. "He drove me always," says Marbury. "He put his soul into me so I could succeed."

More important than Marbury's tattoos or even his complete game is his sturdy confidence. He is a fearless "floor general." Here he was, in just his third year in the league, barely twenty-two years old, shouting instructions

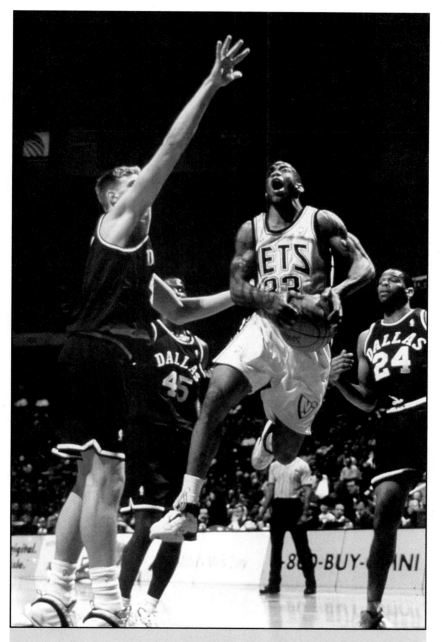

Stephon Marbury fights his way through three Dallas Mavericks before reaching the basket. In his first home game with New Jersey, many of his relatives were in attendance.

like a ten-year veteran—when to trap, when to bump the Mavericks' cutters, when to push the ball or slow it down. His older teammates listened. They were desperate for someone like him. "He's going to be a great leader," said veteran Kendall Gill. "He's young, but all the qualities are there. And we sure needed something. It's good to have somebody come in and be all excited."

The Mavericks spent most of the first half double-teaming Marbury at halfcourt to force him to give up the ball. The strategy worked for awhile as the Mavs built a lead that grew as large as twelve points midway through the second quarter. But Marbury had an answer. He switched from being the point guard to being the shooting guard. Teammates Kerry Kittles and Doug Overton took turns dribbling the ball upcourt, while Marbury ran off screens to get open. They passed the ball back to him, and now he could direct the offense. He used crossover dribbles to free up space to drive to the basket or pass to an open teammate. With 30 seconds left in the half, he lobbed a pass to Keith Van Horn. When the tall forward got fouled and made one free throw, the Nets had their first lead in a game in more than a week. They scored once more to take a 42–39 lead into the locker room at the half.

The Nets were so hungry for a victory that they brought in famous motivational speaker Tony Robbins for a halftime pep talk. Then the New Jersey coaches devised more tricky plays for Marbury to overcome the Dallas double-teaming. "They were great with the chalkboard," Marbury said. The plays to free up Marbury worked so well that Dallas abandoned their double-team strategy midway through the third quarter. When Marbury launched a 35-footer at the third-quarter buzzer, the ball swished through the hoop. And the Nets had their largest lead of the game, 67–60. Marbury flapped his arms to the crowd, urging

Before he was traded to the Nets, Marbury starred with the Minnesota Timberwolves. Here, he goes in for an uncontested layup against the Los Angeles Lakers.

them to cheer, as his family and friends behind the bench went crazy.

Nothing rattled Marbury in the critical fourth quarter. For every charge the Mavericks made, he had an answer. The Nets were ahead by five points when Mavs sharpshooter Hubert Davis hit three straight three-pointers to put Dallas ahead, 79–75. With less than five minutes to go, the Nets desperately needed to score to break the Dallas momentum. At the New Jersey bench during a timeout, it was not coach Don Casey designing the crucial play, it was the team's young point guard. Marbury suggested that the Nets try the old "UCLA cut," where the point guard passes and runs through a screen to get the ball back. The coach listened. "He knows the game," Casey would say. On the floor, Marbury dished the ball in deep, took the return pass as he glided to the hoop, and laid it in. The teams exchanged baskets three more times. At the tail end of the exchange, Michael Finley's slam dunk for Dallas and Keith Van Horn's jumper for the Nets made the score 85–83.

With a minute remaining and the Nets trailing by a basket, Marbury walked up the court, pounding the ball up and down like a heavy metal drummer. In the stands, brother Donnie said, "He's going to drive here." Sure enough, Marbury blew by Finley and drove down the lane. He put up a high-arcing scoop that fell through the basket with 57.1 seconds left. And he was fouled on the play. "I called it!" screamed Donnie above the crowd's roar. "I told you, didn't I? He's been doing that since he's been a baby." Then Marbury calmly sank the free throw to give the Nets a one-point lead.

The Mavericks did not give up. Dallas power forward Gary Trent backed in on Jayson Williams and hit a jumper over him to take back the lead, 87–86. Only 38 seconds remained. As the clock ticked down, Marbury dribbled near the top of the key. He looked to pass to a teammate, but no one was open. Perhaps Marbury did not mind. Maybe he wanted to take the shot himself. All the great ones do. He found a crease, drove down the lane, and threw a floater toward the hoop. It rimmed out. But Kittles was under the basket to grab the rebound for the Nets. He tried to shoot and was fouled.

Only 17 seconds remained as Kittles stepped to the line for two free throws. Marbury offered encouragement to his teammate. Kittles needed it. He had missed six of eight shots in the game, including an embarrassing airball. With Marbury's encouragement, Kittles sank the first free throw to tie the game. The Mavericks called a timeout to try to fluster him. Then they called a second timeout. The fans were chanting "Let's go, Nets!—Let's go, Nets!" As the teams returned to the court, and Kittles toed the line, Marbury put his finger to his lips to shush the crowd. He wanted silence for his teammate. The crowd obliged. Kittles nailed the second free throw to give the Nets the lead, 88–87.

The Mavericks rushed down the court for one last shot. Above the crowd's roar, Marbury shouted defensive instructions. New Jersey's suffocating defense gave Dallas nothing. Finley was forced to throw up an off-balance six-teen-footer. The ball clanked off the rim. The buzzer sounded. Marbury jumped into Jayson Williams's arms and raised his fist. Confetti rained down from the stands. Marbury's family and friends danced in the aisles as they watched their favorite player run crazily around the court with his new teammates. Marbury escorted the players into the locker room by crashing open the swinging doors and shouting "Yeah, bay-bee!" He had scored a team-high 29 points, but he had led the team in so many other ways, too.

Then Marbury threw a pizza party. He ordered several pizzas to be delivered to the Nets' locker room—*the winning* locker room. "That's the perfect homecoming," he

Marbury (far right) poses with teammates (left to right) Keith Van Horn, Kendall Gill, and Kerry Kittles. When the Nets defeated the Mavericks in Marbury's home debut, Kittles's two free throws helped seal the victory.

said as reporters gathered around his locker. "I don't care if we had been playing a high school team. Whatever it takes to get this team's confidence up. We got the job done and that's something right now."

The Nets were not fooling themselves. They knew this was just their fourth win in 22 games. They did not consider themselves a playoff threat—yet. "But I am excited," said Jayson Williams, who pointed to Marbury. "We have a little guy over there who can put the ball in the basket." Kendall Gill was even more complimentary. "He's got a ton of confidence and he's a natural leader," said Gill.

"He's already taken the team over. He reminds me a lot of Isiah Thomas in the way he plays and how he takes charge of everything."

Marbury had eaten half a pizza and was seated with ice bags wrapped around his legs. He talked of New Jersey's opportunity to become a dominant NBA team in the twenty-first century. "I'm an energy player. I can't play passive like this team has been," said Marbury. "I know that in due time, we'll start selling out. Nothing will happen overnight. People will want to see us play. We are going to become a team that is really exciting."

Chapter 2

Coney Island's Finest

At the southern tip of Brooklyn is a small piece of land called Coney Island. It is surrounded on three sides by New York City's Lower Bay and the Atlantic Ocean and on its east side by Brighton Beach. It is not completely surrounded by water, so technically speaking it is not a true island. But most of its residents feel as isolated from the rest of the world as if stranded alone on a deserted island in the middle of the ocean. The tourists who stroll along the boardwalk of the old famous amusement park do not see the harsh life on Coney Island's streets. Just beyond the aging merry-go-rounds and other rides is a long stretch of decayed buildings marked by graffiti and bullet holes and hardship.

The high-rise government housing projects that run for twenty blocks are infested with drugs and gangs. "Having lived in poverty, I know where I'm from," says Marbury. "I'm from the ghetto. I think that made me stronger and tougher." But life on Coney Island is not just sorrow. There is love among the people who live there,.and the air is often filled with laughter. For many there is pride and hope for the future. "There are drugs and shootings in the projects," Marbury says, "but you can't let anything keep you from your dreams."

Born on February 20, 1977, Stephon grew up in a

four-bedroom apartment on the fourth floor of a fifteen-story high-rise on Coney Island's West 31st Street between Surf Avenue and Mermaid Avenue. The building is called the Surfside Gardens projects, and from the outside it looks today much as it did then, a run-down concrete structure littered with empty and broken bottles in paper sacks. Wailing police sirens fill the air, and occasional cracks of gunfire pierce the darkness.

Stephon's father, Donald Marbury, is a construction laborer who often struggled to find work during Stephon's youth. Mabel Marbury, Stephon's mother, worked as a day-care worker. While both parents loved Stephon and the other children, Donald served as the disciplinarian. "We have a working agreement, my wife and I," said Donald when Stephon was still a teenager. "If there's something positive, that's hers. If there's something difficult—a problem—I take care of it."

Stephon has two older twin sisters, Stephanie and Marcia. Both were warm and loving to young Stephon. Marcia grew up to be an education reporter for a television station. Stephanie became an elementary school special education teacher's aide. When Stephanie was twelve years old, she begged her mother to name the new baby after her, and in return she would raise him. So, when the baby was born, he was named Stephon Xzavier Marbury. Stephanie lived up to her promise, raising Stephon, and sometimes being mistaken for his mother. She fed him, bathed him, and comforted him. When he fell off his bicycle as a youngster, she closed the wound that is now a scar on his right leg. "We have a special bond," said Stephanie. "He is my namesake."

Stephon developed his soft side from his mother and sisters. From his brothers he learned the art of basketball. It is the sport of choice in his town. As one playground coach puts it, "Basketball is all we got. There ain't nothing

Marbury attempts to shoot over the outstretched arm of San Antonio's Chuck Person. Marbury's road to the NBA was not easy. Although his neighborhood was infested with drugs and violence, he did not lose focus.

else to do in Coney Island." Stephon has three older brothers and one younger, and all of them took basketball quite seriously. There was great pressure on the brothers to make it to the NBA and lead the family out of poverty. When Stephon was a newborn, his oldest brother, Eric, lifted him from his cradle, held him aloft, and announced, "There's something special about this one. God sends truly great players to us once every ten years. This will be one of the greatest players who ever lived."

Eric did his best to fulfill his prophecy himself. He was seventeen years older than Stephon. When Eric graduated from Lincoln High School, he attended the University of Georgia on a basketball scholarship. He played guard for the Georgia Bulldogs where he teamed with future NBA players Dominique Wilkins and Vern Fleming. But he fell just short of becoming a pro when he was cut in training camp in 1982 by the San Diego (now Los Angeles) Clippers. Eric is now an ironworker living in Brooklyn. "I didn't make the NBA for whatever reason—maybe I wasn't good enough," said Eric. "But ever since my brothers were small, I made sure they all knew the commitment it would take."

Eric worked first with Donnie, who was five years younger. Since Eric's nickname in Coney Island was Sky Dog, the locals began calling Donnie "Sky Pup." Under Eric's watchful eye, Sky Pup developed good basketball skills and attended Texas A&M where he played for two years. In 1986 he led the Southwest Conference in scoring. But he was bypassed by the NBA, and his basketball career ended. Next up was Norman, twelve years younger than Eric. Norman's nickname was Jou-Jou, and some say his skills were good enough to make it to the pros. But Jou-Jou struggled with his studies. He played for only one year at St. Francis College in Brooklyn. At that point, the family had a reputation in Coney Island as blacktop wizards with

After venturing into the lane, Marbury attempts to avoid Nate McMillan of the Seattle SuperSonics.

little hope for the NBA. Stephon had a burning desire to change that. Stephon's cousin, Jamel Thomas, said, "People would say, 'He's just another Marbury who ain't gonna make it.' Stephon would be like, 'Uh-huh.' He'd use that."

Stephon learned his moves on a patch of blacktop called The Garden, named in honor of Madison Square Garden, the home of the NBA's New York Knicks. At age three, he was outplaying neighborhood kids twice his age. That spring he was driven by his father to the University of Georgia to see brother Eric practice and play. During a break in practice, little Stephon picked up a basketball, dribbled upcourt, and started making basket after basket. Stephon paid attention to everything his older brothers did, just as his younger brother, Zack, later did as he watched Stephon. "Everything my brothers did to prepare themselves to reach the next level, I did," said Stephon. "I'm a mixture of all my brothers, their work ethics, their talents, into one."

But while Stephon credits all his brothers, it was Eric who pushed him the hardest. Eric designed an exhausting training regimen for Stephon. He made his little brother run up and down the fifteen flights of stairs in the housing project, three times per workout. Then he led him across Surf Avenue and the boardwalk to run sprints in Coney Island's sand. "I knew everything Eric told me would make me better," said Stephon, who learned other valuable things from his brother—martial arts and the importance of studying in school and getting good grades.

By age nine, Stephon could dribble expertly with either hand and had developed such a solid shot that he staged shooting exhibitions at halftime during Lincoln High School games. A year later he was gliding through the air at The Garden, showing opponents the bottoms of his shoes on his way to the basket. In 1988, the annual

Marbury whips the ball behind a defender to a trailing teammate.
Marbury learned quite a bit from his older brothers Eric, Donnie,
and Norman. Eric, the oldest, was especially influential.

recruiting guide *Hoop Scoop* called him the best sixth-grader in the nation. He wrote a letter to his mother, promising her a "nice, big ol' house" and telling her to "just remember that you borne a star."

Stephon starred on the school team at Intermediate School 238. As an eighth-grader, he once sneaked into a local camp for high schoolers. He played so well that when officials discovered he was underage, they let him stay anyway. He told anyone who would listen, "I'm going to be an NBA star." At age thirteen, he watched brother Norman and his Lincoln High Railsplitters lose a state tournament game. Stephon cried his eyes out. "Even when it wasn't his game, his team losing made him cry," said the coach. Stephon vowed that when he joined the Lincoln team, he would lead the Railsplitters to the city and state title. Upon entering high school the following year, Stephon had the panther tattoo etched into his arm. "The panther is quick and smart and always alert to everything," he explained. "He's sitting on top of a mountain, with the sun and the clouds. That's where I want to see myself."

A reporter who came to Coney Island to write about the basketball being played there, asked Stephon about college. Stephon said he would like to play at Syracuse University, "because at Syracuse, you play in front of 32,820 people every home game. It's crazy-loud in there." Stephon had not yet even dribbled a ball in high school, and he was already thinking about college. He had a plan. And a purpose. "It was my whole dream," he said, "to take my mother out of the projects."

Chapter 3

The Railsplitters

Stephon was five-feet ten-inches and a wiry 140 pounds when he entered Abraham Lincoln High School on Ocean Parkway. His enrollment ended a recruiting war among area schools bidding for his talents. "A couple of the Catholic schools really wanted me, but I think they knew all along I'd be coming here," Stephon said. "It seems like yesterday that I was a little kid coming to the games, wishing I could play for Lincoln. This is home."

Basketball coach Bobby Hartstein had already seen Stephon's super moves on the court. He immediately put Stephon at point guard on the varsity team, the Railsplitters. Hartstein had coached all the Marburys, along with at least a dozen cousins, as Lincoln established a fine reputation for boys' basketball in New York City. "Schools say they have basketball teams," said Hartstein. "We like to say we have a basketball program." Rival coaches were jealous of Lincoln's success. "Team, *program*, whatever," said one New York City coach. "Bobby does a real nice job, but it hasn't hurt to have gotten all those Marburys."

Stephon took jersey number three, as had all the Marbury brothers before him, in honor of Eric, who wore it first. To the Marburys, the number three represented extraordinary vision on the court, as if they had a third eye.

As a freshman at Lincoln High, Stephon led a team of college-bound seniors, including big forward Tchaka Shipp, who was headed for Seton Hall. Stephon felt comfortable from the start, playing nearly every minute of every game. In a performance typical of his first season, he scored 8 of his team's last 10 points in a thrilling 58–55 victory over Lafayette High. "Did you see that jump shot the Marbury kid made off the dribble?" asked the Lafayette coach as he shook his head in disbelief. Stephon's response? "I like the pressure," he said.

Stephon adjusted well in the classroom, too, and even made the math honor roll. He was comfortable with high school life. "The drug dealers never even bothered Stephon," said coach Hartstein. "Hey, they wanted him to make it, too." Lincoln reached the quarterfinals of the Public Schools Athletic League Division A playoffs before that season ended. A winter's worth of games around New York City had given Stephon a chance to showcase his talent. A respected college scout named Tom Konchalski echoed the opinion of others in the area when he said, "Along with Kenny Anderson and Pearl Washington, he's one of the best freshman point guards I've ever seen."

One day Stephon placed a telephone call to a boy named Kevin Garnett. Kevin was a schoolboy superstar in South Carolina whom Stephon had seen on a national high school highlights show on television. Kevin was a tall center who could dribble like a guard. "Wow, I was thinking, for a big man, that wasn't normal," Stephon recalled. So Stephon called Kevin, just to meet him on the phone. Kevin's mother answered. She recognized the name Stephon Marbury right away. "I saw you in the magazines," Mrs. Garnett said. "You're that cute little fellow." Kevin was out playing basketball, so Stephon left his telephone number. When Kevin came home later that day, he tried calling Stephon. "Sure, I'd heard about this kid in New

Marbury tries to get the crowd involved. He started wearing number three in high school because his brothers had worn it. He did not switch to number thirty-three until he reached New Jersey, which had retired number three in honor of the deceased Drazen Petrovic.

York, Mayberry," said Kevin. "Can't shoot well, but that mother's fast." Kevin tried over and over again to reach Stephon, but Stephon was never home. "It was like trying to get in touch with the President of the United States," said Kevin. Finally they connected. "Yo, boy," said Stephon.

"Who's this?" said Kevin.

"It's Steph, man."

"Mayberry . . . uh, Marbury?"

"Yeah."

"Yeah?"

"Yeah."

"I been reading about you . . . "

They became instant phone buddies. Kevin rang up eighty dollars worth of calls one month, fifty-five dollars another. He had to give half his paycheck from his part-time job at Burger King to his mother to pay for the calls. "One night I was eavesdropping on them," said Shirley Garnett, "and it was all 'Yeah, man, know this?' and 'Yeah, man, know that?' For hours. Stephon was a real inspiration in Kevin's life. Stephon served as a listener, someone who was there for Kevin in a tough time."

Stephon changed too. There is a fine line between confidence and bragging, and Stephon often crossed that line. He taunted opponents with trash-talking and finger-pointing. Such childish behavior finally ended his sophomore year. "I learned to treat everybody with respect," he said. "When you're a good person, good things happen to you." Sure enough, good things happened to Stephon and his Lincoln High teammates that year. The Railsplitters steamrolled into the PSAL playoffs on the strength of Stephon's shooting and passing. He averaged 22.5 points and 7.5 assists a game while shooting a blistering 43 percent from three-point range. The Railsplitters cruised through the playoffs to the semifinal game where they met rival Grady High from Brighton Beach. The game was no contest. Stephon hit 9 of 15 shots from the floor, including 4 of 6 three-pointers, to score 24 points, as Lincoln won in a rout, 57–44. Unfortunately, though, Stephon crashed into a Grady player late in the game. He suffered a hip pointer, a deep bruise to the hip or the muscles attached to it.

The pain from the hip pointer was still with Marbury five days later when he arrived with his teammates at Madison Square Garden for the PSAL championship. When he stepped onto the shiny wooden floor with the Knicks logo he forgot all about his aching hip. But as soon as the game started, the pain came shooting back. The Railsplitters jumped out to a 9–5 lead over top-seeded Walton High from the Bronx, but the Wildcats scored the next 13 points to take control of the game. Walton went on to win, 66–60. Jamel Thomas, Stephon's cousin, led the Railsplitters with 19 points and 13 rebounds. But Stephon could hardly contribute and finished with five points.

College recruiters had been talking to Stephon since seventh grade, but now that he was a junior, they were hounding him—calling him at home and at school, showing up at The Garden in Coney Island, begging him to accept athletic scholarships. Stephon had grown to a full six feet, two inches, and maintained a solid grade point average of 2.75. He was among the most heavily recruited sixteen-year-olds in the country. The swirl in Coney Island settled some when he announced he had narrowed his university choices to four—Syracuse, Minnesota, Georgia Tech, and UCLA.

Stephon led the Railsplitters to the Public Schools Athletic League championship game again, but for the second year in a row his team's season ended in sorrow. Stephon skipped onto the court at Madison Square Garden amid chants of "You the man, Stephon, you the man!" from many in the crowd of 9,520. After the game,

Marbury proudly displays the two tattoos on his left arm. The top tattoo says, "Coney Island's Finest." Beneath that is a drawing of Marbury hugging his daughter, Stephanie, and the words "Love of my life."

however, he lay flat on his back with his hands covering his eyes, crying uncontrollably. His team had lost, 73–66, to Manhattan's Martin Luther King High. And as in the PSAL final of the year before, Stephon did not play well. He scored 17 points, but he made just five of 24 shots, and he turned the ball over six times. "I didn't play up to my capabilities tonight," he said later after he got himself under control. "I wanted to get my team more involved, and I think I just tried too hard. We didn't execute our game plan."

Stephon was more determined than ever to win a title. He had just one chance left. He filled his summer with hoops, playing on a club team called the East Harlem Gauchos, and leading it to several tournament titles. He played on the junior national team where he trained for two weeks in Minnesota before leaving for the Junior World Games in Argentina. He had lived his life in the pulse of a big city, and so his time in Minnesota felt awkward.

"I hated the place. And that was in the summer," he said. "It was culture shock. By the time we were done, I couldn't wait to go to Argentina, and whoever thought I'd say that?" At the Junior World Games in Buenos Aires, Stephon led the U.S. team on an undefeated march to the title.

Stephon's favorite moment of that summer came when he went to Chicago where Kevin Garnett had just moved. He finally got to meet his phone buddy Kevin, outside a West Side gym. "What's up," Stephon said.

"Ready?" Kevin replied.

"Yeah, I'm ready."

"Let's go play some ball."

They shook hands, hugged, and walked inside. In a pickup game against older players, Stephon walked the ball up for the first play, dribbled at the top of the key, and waited for his phone buddy to make his move. "It was almost like I could hear Steph saying, 'Spin. Spin. I'm

Marbury takes a layup as two Phoenix Suns helplessly watch. While in high school, Marbury called Kevin Garnett even though they had never met. They quickly became friends and eventually starred together on the Timberwolves.

waiting on you,'" said Kevin. "I could feel it. Spin. Spin." Kevin spun toward the hoop, Stephon threw a perfect lob above the rim, and Kevin caught it and slammed it home with a thunderous yell. "The people in there went crazy," says Garnett. "People ran. They were running out of the building. They had never seen something like that."

Stephon returned to New York City and tuned up for his final high school season by leading his club team, the Gauchos, to a few more tournament titles. "He's lucky to have his brothers behind him," said club coach Ronnie Naclerio. "They're the ones who keep the kid on the straight and narrow. If he doesn't practice hard one day, Don or Eric tells him, 'Look, I loafed in practice. And look what happened to me.'"

Stephon was averaging nearly 30 points and 10 assists a game midway through his senior season at Lincoln. There was talk that he was the best high school player at any position in the country. But Stephon was already thinking ahead to college. He talked nearly every night with his teammate and pal, Jason "Juice" Sowell, about which university might be best for him. Together Stephon and Juice shared dreams of someday making it in the NBA. Who knows? Maybe they would end up playing together on the same team.

Eventually Stephon decided he wanted to attend Georgia Tech. He knew of another New York City guard named Kenny Anderson who starred in the NBA after playing for the Yellow Jackets. "Georgia Tech really knows how to treat its point guards," he would say to Juice. But Stephon's brothers clamored for him to pick Syracuse. For weeks he agonized over what to do. He had always listened to his brothers. But he really wanted to go to Georgia Tech. Finally one day, his sister Stephanie wiped the tears from his eyes and said, "If you really want to go there, go there."

Other high school players were already making their

decisions, and newspaper reporters were hounding Stephon for his choice. So Stephon and Lincoln's Coach Hartstein arranged for a press conference at a restaurant in the Bay Ridge section of Brooklyn. With his family surrounding him, Stephon announced his decision to the media. "I just feel that Georgia Tech is better for me, a great opportunity," he said. "The guys, when I went down there for my visit, treated me with a lot of respect, like I was one of the best point guards in the country. I'm not saying Syracuse didn't treat me with respect. I just felt more comfortable with Georgia Tech."

Meanwhile, Lincoln was ranked No. 10 in the nation midway through the season, with only a single loss to California power Mater Dei High, a game in which Stephon scored 39 points. The Railsplitters lost just twice more through the regular season and went as high as No. 4 in the country. For the season, Stephon averaged 28 points, 9.5 assists, and 3.5 steals. None of that was important now. Stephon desperately wanted a city championship. But such thoughts were put on hold for something even more important. Two weeks after his eighteenth birthday, Stephon became a father. His girlfriend, Nicole Thompson, gave birth to a girl. The baby was named Stephanie. "The light of my eyes," Stephon called her.

Lincoln rolled through the playoffs, including a second-round 91–42 thumping of Clinton High, and a quarterfinal 71–56 victory over Boys & Girls High in which Stephon scored 28 points. Then the Railsplitters got past Manhattan High, 56–50, to earn their third straight trip to Madison Square Garden. "This title is definitely the one that I want, the one that I dream about," Stephon said at the news conference the day before the game. "I had three chances. I've come up short three times. Hopefully, this year I'll come up and win." With Georgia Tech coach Bobby Cremins among the 8,842 fans at the game the next

After narrowing his college choices to Syracuse, Minnesota, Georgia Tech, and UCLA, Marbury finally announced that he would attend Georgia Tech. "I just felt that Georgia Tech is better for me, a great opportunity," he said.

day, Stephon became the first Marbury to lead Lincoln to a city title. Against taller Robeson High from Brooklyn, Stephon's cousin Jamel Thomas crashed the boards for 17 rebounds, while Stephon's backcourt mate, Gerald Hawkins, poured in 21 points.

But the hero was Stephon. He scored 26 points and repeatedly kept the Railsplitters in the game. His team trailed with 7:15 left in the fourth quarter when he drained a three-pointer to tie it, 40–40. He hit two jumpers and three short runners down the stretch to give Lincoln several slim leads. In the waning seconds, as the Railsplitters desperately clinged to a 57–56 lead, the ball was in Stephon's hands again. With 11 seconds left, he was fouled. He stepped to the free throw line with the weight of his team, his school, all of Coney Island, on his shoulders. First free throw—up . . . good! Second free throw—up . . . good! Robeson High sharpshooter Todd Myles missed a three-pointer with five seconds left, and Lincoln closed it out with two more free throws for a 61–56 victory. The horn sounded with Stephon's family crying in the stands and Stephon getting mobbed by his teammates. "I've got everything now!" he screamed. "I've got everything now!"

But more was coming. First he was named the playoff tournament's Most Valuable Player. The next day he was named Mr. New York Basketball. Then, he was picked as the National High School Player of the Year. "I consider this my best individual award," he announced at a press conference at the New York Hilton. Finally, he scored 21 points in his last high school game as he lead the Railsplitters to the New York state championship. His next stop was college. "I'm really looking forward to playing at Georgia Tech next year," he said. "I've got a million more games to play."

Chapter 4

Yellow Jackets and Timberwolves

Stephon Marbury spent most of the spring and summer of 1995 on a happy cloud. He played on the East squad in the classic McDonald's All-American High School Basketball Game against his phone pal Kevin Garnett who played for the West. The game was played in St. Louis, and Stephon scored 11 points and led all players with 10 assists. But Garnett scored 18 points and grabbed 11 rebounds to lead the West to a 126–115 victory. Then Marbury joined his club team on its way to France for a series of international games. Finally he helped the U.S. team win the junior world championships in Greece.

Marbury drifted happily atop his cloud into August and on to Georgia Tech. Then, suddenly, the cloud burst with a thunderclap. Jason "Juice" Sowell was dead. Stephon's friend was gunned down on Coney Island's mean streets, apparently the victim of a random shooting by gang members. Juice was buried in the cold Brooklyn ground, and a mural of him was painted on a Coney Island building with the words "Shoot hoops, not guns."

Lincoln's Coach Bobby Hartstein went to visit Marbury at Georgia Tech soon after. He saw that Marbury had turned his dorm room into a shrine for Juice. Pictures of his fallen friend were everywhere. The coach helped Marbury in his grief. So did Stephanie, who called her brother every day. Stephon gradually came out of his depression. He was heartened by the success of his phone buddy Kevin Garnett, who had skipped college and gone straight to the NBA. Garnett was busy adjusting to life with the Minnesota Timberwolves, and Marbury was learning the college game, yet the two young men found time to talk often. "When he had 21 (points against the Vancouver Grizzlies), I was telling people, 'He's going off, he's snapping,'" said Marbury. "Guys would say, 'Yeah, yeah, Garnett's all right.' I'm like, 'Watch. Watch.'" Garnett admired Marbury too, and he bragged about his buddy to Timberwolves coach Flip Saunders. "Georgia Tech's going to play Manhattan," said Garnett, "and I tell Flip, 'My boy's about to play. Better get a seat belt. My boy's got a game.'"

Garnett and the rest of the Timberwolves were in the national television audience that watched Marbury's college debut against Manhattan at the Georgia Dome in Atlanta. With 8,411 in the stands, including Marbury's parents who were seated at courtside, Marbury put on a brilliant show with 16 points, 5 assists, and 4 steals. The Yellow Jackets won with ease, 87–67. Marbury's performance was even more amazing when the forty-two reporters who surrounded him at his locker afterward found out he had tonsillitis and a fever of 102 degrees. "I wasn't really focused at all," said Marbury, who took an antibiotic injection before the game. "I was weak today. I could have played better."

The Yellow Jackets, ranked No. 25 in the polls, flew north to New York City in late November to play the fifth-ranked Georgetown Hoyas at Madison Square Garden. Marbury returned to his home in Coney Island where he

When Marbury reached Georgia Tech, he felt as if he were on top of the world. His emotions suddenly came tumbling down when his friend Jason "Juice" Sowell was shot and killed on Coney Island.

would stay through Thanksgiving. "I love college," he said. "The only thing missing is mom and home-cooked meals." The game between Georgia Tech and Georgetown was billed as a showdown between Marbury and the Hoyas' lightning-quick sophomore, Allen Iverson. Marbury assured reporters that he would not allow the game to become a one-on-one battle. "When someone scores on you, your first instinct is to go after him," he admitted. "But this is a team thing. He's going to get his and I'm going to get mine, regardless."

Marbury was right. Iverson finished with 23 points, 6 assists, and 2 steals. Marbury had 13 points, 8 assists, and 7 steals. One veteran reporter wrote, "Marbury was the more spectacular player." Georgetown, however, had the better team, and in front of a boisterous crowd of 15,249, the Hoyas pulled away to a 94–72 win. "He's a great player, but he's a freshman," Iverson said about Marbury. "He's got a lot to learn, just as I've got a lot to learn. He'll get better."

Marbury returned to the area just before Christmas when his Yellow Jackets met top-ranked Massachusetts at the Meadowlands in New Jersey. His parents and brothers and sisters were in the stands again, cheering and having fun. "Shoot that, Steph!" yelled Eric. "This is where you take over, Steph!" When Marbury made a spectacular steal and breakaway layup, Donnie shouted, "What did I tell you? The steal! I know my little brother!" But Marbury made just 7 of 20 shots, and Georgia Tech lost, 75–67. "He's playing nervous because of the expectations," Georgia Tech coach Bobby Cremins said about his young freshman. "He's the most scrutinized athlete that I think I've ever seen. There's just too much publicity regarding Stephon Marbury. I wish he'd just be left alone and be a normal student athlete."

Through December and January, Marbury continued

Marbury made an immediate impact when he reached Georgia Tech. In his debut against Manhattan, Marbury scored 16 points, handed out 5 assists, and collected 4 steals to lead the Yellow Jackets to a 87–67 victory.

to show glimpses of brilliance, but too often he tried too hard and made bad decisions or disappeared altogether. Against powerful University of Kentucky, he scored 17 points in the first half to give the Yellow Jackets a surprising lead. But in the second half, he did not score a single point as the Wildcats surged to victory. Against mighty Duke, he managed just four points in the first half, but then took over the game in the second half with 23 points to lead Tech to an 86–81 win. At home against Mount St. Mary's, with his team up by one point with a minute to play. Marbury foolishly threw a blind wraparound pass out-of-bounds that cost his team the game. "We don't need to be forcing it in a close game like that," said senior guard Drew Barry. "Stephon's a great talent. He's going to be a great player. But right now he has a lot to learn." Marbury accepted the blame. He was determined to improve. He asked for a tape of that game, the only player to do so. He stayed up until 3:30 A.M. watching it.

Marbury's greatness continued emerge. He scored 24 points and prevented his counterpart Harold Deane from scoring a single basket in a key Atlantic Coast Conference victory over Virginia. He hit a pressure 12-footer in the lane with 42 seconds left in overtime to beat Duke by a basket. Three days later at Chapel Hill, he hit a driving jumper along the baseline with 33 seconds left to force overtime against North Carolina. Then he made a crucial basket, steal, and blocked shot in overtime to carry his team to another win. "He's not looking to score points as much as he's looking to pass the ball now," teammate Barry said. "Everybody knows he can score. Now he looks like a real pure point guard."

Many claimed that Marbury was already good enough for the next level. They said he and his family were ready for a rich NBA contract. Asked if he would consider turning professional after just one season in college,

Marbury replied, "If I'm guaranteed to be in the lottery (among the top picks in the draft), I wouldn't even hesitate. I'm leaving. In fact, I would hope the people at Georgia Tech would tell me to leave." Talk began to swirl that Marbury might go pro. Coach Cremins hoped it was not so. "There's a lot of talk about Stephon's making it to the NBA for his family," said the coach. "But his mother once told me, 'We're a family, and we're going to be a family whether he makes it to the NBA or not.' And they're a happy family. They could live there (in Coney Island) the rest of their lives and be happy."

Meanwhile, Marbury was driving Tech to its first regular season ACC title. He scored 24 points to beat Tim Duncan's eighth-ranked Wake Forest Demon Deacons. Then he scored 18 more over Clemson as the Yellow Jackets finished 20–10 overall and 13–3 in the conference to claim the title. "That's why I came to Georgia Tech, to be an impact player and change the program around," said Marbury. "I think I've done everything to be an impact player. I'm accomplishing my goal and also helping the team." Up in Minnesota, Kevin Garnett was bragging up his phone buddy. The Timberwolves had the fifth pick in the upcoming NBA draft, and general manager Kevin McHale was excited. "KG, come into my office," he would say to Garnett. "Is your boy coming out? KG, talk to me. Is he coming out?"

In the ACC Tournament, Marbury led Georgia Tech past North Carolina State, Maryland, and Wake Forest to win the title. The media seemed more interested in Marbury's decision about turning pro. "When it's time to go, I'll know," he said. "The NBA is a lot easier than college. In college you have strict defenses. The NBA is a lot of one on one. That's pretty much what my game is—one on one, breaking down players and defending."

Marbury knew he was headed to the pros. He just did

As Marbury's freshman year progressed, he continued to improve. He played like a veteran, leading Georgia Tech to key victories over traditional ACC powers North Carolina and Duke.

not think it was fair to announce it publicly until his season with his Georgia Tech teammates was over. The Yellow Jackets were appearing in their first NCAA Tournament in three years, and Marbury wanted to see how far he could lead them. After an easy first-round win in the Southeast Region, the Yellow Jackets faced Boston College. With the national spotlight shining now, Marbury kicked it into a higher gear. He scored a career-high 29 points on 10-of-12 shooting, including 6-of-7 from three-point range. He also had 4 rebounds, 6 assists, and 2 steals as Georgia Tech rolled to a 102–89 victory. The Yellow Jackets had reached the Sweet 16. But their fine season ended there as the stifling defense of the Cincinnati Bearcats stopped them by the score of 87–70. "The shots just weren't there," said Marbury, who managed to lead Georgia Tech with 15 points. "My feet weren't set when it was time to shoot."

It was time for something else, however. Marbury had an announcement to make. A press conference was arranged at Junior's Restaurant on Flatbush Avenue in Brooklyn. His parents and brothers and sisters sat with him, along with Coach Hartstein from Lincoln High and Coach Cremins from Georgia Tech. Marbury told the reporters, "Basically, I just want to say that I've reached my decision. The opportunity that I have right now is really knocking, and I have to take advantage of it. So right now, I just want to say it's official. I'm declaring to come out of college and go to the NBA."

A month later, Marbury and his family were at New Jersey's Continental Airlines Arena with the other top college players and their families for the draft. Which team would pick Marbury? Everyone knew the Philadelphia 76ers would take Allen Iverson with the first pick. The next two teams, Toronto and Vancouver, were not interested in point guards. The Milwaukee Bucks had the fourth pick and needed a guard. The Minnesota Timberwolves picked

Marbury kicks the ball out to the perimeter after he encounters three defenders near the basket. Marbury made the jump to the NBA after only one season at Georgia Tech.

fifth. Marbury wished he could play with his pal Kevin Garnett and the Wolves, but he had heard that the Bucks wanted him too. What he did not know was that Kevin McHale was making a secret trade with the Bucks at that very moment. If there were no surprises with the first three picks, Milwaukee would select Marbury and then Minnesota would draft Connecticut guard Ray Allen. Then the teams would swap players, with Minnesota also giving Milwaukee a future first-round pick. But for Marbury and his family, at this moment, simply making it to the NBA was pure joy.

When the Bucks announced Marbury as their pick, Stephon and his family wept openly. "People have been telling me that I would play in the NBA since I was this high," Stephon said, holding his hand at his waist. Then he was handed a Milwaukee Bucks baseball cap that he proudly put on his head. Oldest brother Eric cried and said, "For twenty years we waited for this day, and now it's here. Me and Donnie probably made our mistakes and Norman probably made his mistakes, but we didn't make any mistakes with this one. No matter what happened, we never stopped believing that one of us was destined to go. We all wore number 3, and now number 3 is in the NBA."

Ray Allen was selected by Minnesota as part of the secret plan, and for another half an hour the draft moved merrily along. Then an NBA official approached Marbury and told him to switch caps with Allen. Marbury was confused. Then he heard the announcement. The Wolves had traded for him. He would be playing in Minnesota. Playing with Garnett. "I'm a Timberwolf!" he shouted as he smiled for a photographer. Bucks fans watching the draft at Milwaukee's arena booed when the trade was announced. But McHale and the Timberwolves were celebrating. "Stephon can flat-out play," said McHale. "To me, it's like a great quarterback. If you get a great quarterback, you can win any game you're in. His ability to take over games reminds me of that. This guy is going to be a great player."

Chapter 5

Playoff Hopes

"Momma, hurry up," Stephon said on the telephone. "I want you to be in that new house by Christmas." Marbury had signed a three-year contract for nearly six million dollars. He was rich. Now he wanted to move his parents far from the dangers of Coney Island. He wanted to buy them a big house in a safer neighborhood. "I won't feel my dream is fulfilled," Stephon told his mother, "until I can walk in and see you sitting in that new house." Finally, in the fall, Mabel and Don began searching for a new home. They were not looking to move, but they wanted their son to feel that he helped them. And, sure, they thought, it would be nice to live in a big house. "This is a dream, from when he was a little boy, to buy me a new house," said Mrs. Marbury. "I never really cared if Stephon made it to the NBA, at least not for my sake. I love all of my children, and all they do for me."

The love was enough, but the Marburys moved anyway, to a suburb in Maryland, near Washington, D.C. Stephanie went with them. The boys stayed in Coney Island. Stephon promised to buy them a "nice apartment" in Brooklyn. They declined. "We don't want Stephon to do anything for us," said Eric. "He's 19 and he's made the NBA. There's nothing more he could do for us. He has fulfilled our dreams."

Meanwhile, Marbury moved into a swanky high-rise

apartment in downtown Minneapolis. "I can't believe it," he said. "I'm living in the same complex as doctors and lawyers. I can go to the store and buy anything I want." In return, the Timberwolves hoped Marbury could buy them some victories. The T-Wolves managed just 26 wins in 82 games the previous season. They had some talented players, but they needed a floor general to direct them. After the third practice of the preseason, Head Coach Flip Saunders, a former college point guard himself, asked Marbury to be more assertive. "But these guys are my elders. I can't yell at them," Marbury said. Coach Saunders replied, "When they step on the floor, they don't ask how old you are."

A few weeks later, on the eve of the season opener, Marbury had settled in. "This is unbelievable," he said. "To be able to play where I wanted to play and with who I wanted to play with, this is great." The T-Wolves were equally thankful. General Manager McHale said his rookie was destined for greatness. "He's always asking questions," said McHale. "He has such a desire to be a great basketball player. I can't see him not getting there."

High hopes filled the Target Center as Marbury and the Wolves opened their season at home against the San Antonio Spurs. But just five minutes into the game disaster struck. Stephon went up for a shot, landed awkwardly, and sprained his ankle. He was helped off the court and did not return. The T-Wolves won the game, but Stephon missed the first two weeks of the season. He missed playing at Portland against former Georgia Tech point guard Kenny Anderson and at Madison Square Garden against the Knicks. When he rejoined the team for a game against the Houston Rockets, he quickly showed that he belonged. The T-Wolves lost, but he and Garnett played as if they had radar. They seemed to know what each other were thinking

After getting drafted by the Timberwolves, Marbury became very popular and very wealthy. He used some of his money to move his parents from Coney Island to a new house in Maryland.

as Marbury lobbed passes and Garnett slammed them home. Marbury was the alley—Garnett was the oop.

While Garnett and forward Tom Gugliotta were Minnesota's primary scoring threats, Marbury got his share of points. He led the T-Wolves in scoring in a game for the first time at Denver when he netted 30 points in a 108–103 victory. Against the Phoenix Suns, he scored 21 points and made a brilliant pass to Gugliotta who hit the winning shot at the buzzer. "He's getting better," said Gugliotta afterward. "I give him a lot of credit because when he came here he relied strictly on his talent. Now he's learning that running an offense is something that's necessary. If he thinks he can take his man, he still takes his man. But he's learning to direct people and tell people where to be." In late December, Marbury tossed in a career-high 33 points to lead his team past the mighty Utah Jazz.

Three nights later he guided a stirring comeback win at home over the Knicks. With his friends in Coney Island watching on television, he took over the game in the third quarter by scoring 11 straight points. The Knicks had led by 16 in the quarter, but Marbury brought the T-Wolves all the way back. He finally tied the game on a brilliant play in which he faked out Chris Childs at the top of the key with a crossover dribble, danced past John Starks at the free throw line, and soared over center Patrick Ewing for a twisting layup. When the buzzer sounded to signal the 88–80 Minnesota win, Marbury threw the ball skyward in celebration as the crowd roared.

Marbury was enjoying his new life in the NBA, but not necessarily in Minnesota. He had said in the fall that he liked the Twin Cities because there was little to do there. "This is the perfect place to play basketball," he explained. "No distractions. It enables you to watch a lot of tape." But now in the dead of winter he realized how miserable he was. Outside the Target Center during the game against

Marbury glides past San Antonio's Tim Duncan for a layup. Marbury's transition to the NBA was fairly smooth. In his first season, he scored 30 points to lead Minnesota past Denver. He topped that effort with 33 points in an upset of the Utah Jazz.

the Knicks, for instance, the temperature was 18 degrees below zero. Marbury decided to try to ignore his life outside of basketball. "I'm just concentrating on getting better every day," he said. "By the end of the year, I know I'll be better than I am now."

He played brilliantly in January, three times leading the T-Wolves in scoring, and in most games leading them in assists and steals. He was named NBA Rookie of the Month. But against Toronto, he was accidentally kneed in the thigh and suffered a deep bruise that caused him to miss eight games, including All-Star Weekend in Cleveland in which he had looked forward to starring in the rookie game. "I wanted my family and friends to be able to see me," said Marbury. "It was going to be exciting. Instead, it's really disappointing."

When Marbury returned to the T-Wolves lineup, he led them toward the playoffs. In a classic battle of rookie guards along the way, he squared off against Philadelphia's Allen Iverson and beat the Sixers scorer in every way to win the game, 104–100. Marbury scored more points (24–17), had more assists (9–4), and committed fewer turnovers (2–4). Most important was Marbury's inspiring play in the fourth quarter. The T-Wolves trailed 97–85 when Marbury came in and scored 13 points to rally his team. One NBA coach described Marbury as "Iverson without the turnovers." Marbury shrugged off comparisons. "People are going to make it a rivalry," he said. "Winning Rookie of the Year would be nice, don't get me wrong, but it really doesn't matter. Winning matters more. I want us to make the playoffs."

The Timberwolves did just that, clinching a spot with six games left in the season when Marbury scored 29 to lead them past the Los Angeles Clippers. The T-Wolves finished with just a 40–42 record and qualified as the eighth and last seed, but to the entire Minnesota organization that did not matter. It was the first time the Timberwolves had ever made the playoffs. "It just feels so good to see people here excited," said Marbury. "To hear that we're a team on the rise." Marbury averaged 21.3 points per game in the playoffs to lead the T-Wolves, but they were swept in three games by the Houston Rockets. He finished second to Iverson in the 1997 Rookie of the Year voting. But it was not enough to take the luster off the most successful season in T-Wolves history.

In the off-season, Marbury returned to Atlanta where he worked out every day at Georgia Tech. He went to Coney Island at least once a week to visit his brothers and friends and stopped in Maryland a few times to enjoy

With the help of Marbury's stellar play, the Timberwolves reached the postseason for the first time in franchise history.

seeing his parents in their new home. Mostly, though, it was a summer of running up and down stairs, lifting weights, and shooting jumpers in the gym. When camp opened for the 1997–98 season, his T-Wolves teammates could hardly believe it. "He's gotten bigger," said Doug West. "And it might not be possible, but Steph's gotten faster. He's picked up on his defense. He's making everybody better, getting them open shots. As long as he stays injury-free, I see big things for him this year."

Marbury did not miss a game the entire season. He improved his shooting percentage and scoring average from his rookie year and had more assists and steals. He led Minnesota to its best-ever record, 45–37. Along the way, he poured in a career-high 38 points against the Utah Jazz, made a club-record eight three-pointers against the Seattle SuperSonics, and was the team's leading scorer twenty-six times. And he led the T-Wolves to a victory over Michael Jordan and the champion Chicago Bulls for the first time in franchise history. That was the good news. The bad news was that Marbury was left off the Western Conference roster for the All-Star game at Madison Square Garden by the NBA coaches who vote for the reserves. "I'm going to be pumped for every game the rest of the season, and I don't have to say why," Marbury said. Garnett understood. "You can't knock Steph for being upset. He knows he's better than some of the guys that'll be there." Coach Saunders agreed. "I'd hate to be the guys that have to guard Stephon from here on out."

The other blemish on Marbury's second season was his honesty about disliking the frigid Minnesota winters, and the ugly criticism of him that followed. Midway through the season, Marbury told a magazine writer that he might think twice about re-signing with the T-Wolves after his three-year contract ran out. "The Wolves know Minnesota isn't the greatest place for me," he said. "I'll never say I like living in Minnesota. No one likes living in 20-degree weather all the time, where you have to walk through tunnels to get every place because it's so cold." Minnesotans were outraged that their young T-Wolves superstar could say such things. Marbury was ripped in the local newspapers. He tried to explain himself by telling local reporters, "I love playing with Kevin. I love playing basketball here. I love being here as far as the fans getting into the game. But it's very difficult to live here. Coming from New York City, it's a big difference. I've adjusted, but it's still hard."

When Gugliotta, the team's top scorer, went down in early February with a season-ending injury, all seemed lost. But Marbury lifted the team on his back and carried it to the playoffs. The T-Wolves lost to the SuperSonics in the first game, then shocked Seattle at Key Arena, 98–93, to win their first playoff game in history. Marbury was the reason why. With Garnett bottled up in the first half and managing just two points, Marbury repeatedly buried outside shots to put his team five points ahead at halftime.

The Sonics were forced to stretch their defense to guard Marbury in the second half, and this freed Garnett inside to score 13 points. Still, Marbury continued to shake free from Gary Payton, nicknamed "the Glove" for his close-fitting defense, to finish with a game-high 25 points. The T-Wolves won Game 3 at the Target Center as well, 98–90, snapping a 15-game Sonics winning streak there. Marbury dished out a game-high 11 assists. But the young T-Wolves lost the next two games and their season suddenly ended. "When that buzzer sounded and that last game was over," Marbury said, "I thought about how close we were, but really how far away we were." Marbury had always been able to raise his game to the next level. He realized now that there was still one step left to take— becoming a playoff winner.

Chapter 6

Filling the Nets

The Timberwolves were playoff contenders now. But Marbury wanted more. He thought his team could go far in the 1999 postseason—as far as the championship. "Some of the media members feel that Houston is number one and the Spurs, Lakers, and Utah are contenders and they aren't even mentioning the Timberwolves," he said. "That's fine. It's better for us if they want to think that because we'll just sneak up on 'em." But Marbury and his mates had to wait for their chance. The owners and players were locked in a bitter dispute over players' salaries, and the season was postponed. The trouble surfaced when it was revealed that the T-Wolves gave Kevin Garnett a long-term contract for $126 million. That enormous sum of money so shocked the owners that they decided to set limits. At first, the players refused to accept these limits. The first three months of the season went by as the two sides haggled. Marbury said,

> It was frustrating, but I just tried to stay focused on working out and making myself stronger. . . . I went home and was able to see my mom a lot. It was fun to be home with my parents and see my brothers and sisters. It was kind of weird too. When my daughter was opening up her toys at Christmas, I was kind of shocked that

I was actually there and not playing basketball somewhere.

Finally the dispute was settled. The shortened season began with Marbury playing brilliantly. In a game against the Houston Rockets he scored 40 points, dished out 12 assists, and did not commit a single turnover. He became only the fifth player in NBA history to record at least 40 points and 10 assists without a turnover. But while he loved his team, he yearned to be closer to his New York City home. He knew he would be a free agent at the end of the season. He told coach Saunders in a hotel room in Boston that he did not think he would re-sign with the T-Wolves. Under the new NBA agreement, teams were allowed to offer Marbury a maximum six-year contract for $71 million. The T-Wolves already had offered him that. But for Marbury it was not just the money. He was homesick. He asked to be traded to either his hometown Knicks or Nets, or to the exciting Los Angeles Lakers. Minnesota reluctantly agreed.

On March 11, 1999, while the T-Wolves were at a hotel in Oakland, California, preparing for a game against the Golden State Warriors, Marbury was given the good news. He had been traded to the New Jersey Nets. In a three-way deal that also involved the Milwaukee Bucks, the T-Wolves received point guard Terrell Brandon, forward Brian Evans, and two draft picks. "It's a shame. Quite frankly, it's a shame," said Minnesota owner Glen Taylor. "It wasn't about money. He grew up in the East and wants to play back by his family."

Marbury, naturally, was thrilled with the news. Teammate Chris Carr, who was also included in the deal and destined for New Jersey, said Marbury could not stop smiling. "He came to my hotel room and said, 'Let me carry your bags.' I said, 'You haven't asked to carry my bags

Marbury was very excited when he heard the news that he had been traded to the New Jersey Nets. It meant that he would play closer to home, near his family, and away from Minnesota's harsh winters.

in two years.' So I'm very, very happy for him and thankful he gets to come home and play in front of his family."

Marbury said, "Playing there will be just like being home. I live 30 minutes away," he said. "I'm close to my family. I'm pretty much a mama's boy. For her to be so close is perfect for me." Living near Manhattan growing up, Marbury naturally was a Knicks fan. But he also crossed the bridge to the Meadowlands as a teenager to see the Nets play. "Came to about 15 games," he said. The Nets were losers then, and they had done little since.

Upon joining his new team, Marbury was shocked at how bad they really were. In his debut with his new teammates in Miami, the Heat torched the Nets, 102–76. Two nights later at Toronto, the young Raptors embarrassed them again. "As a team, we need discipline and guidance, and right now, we have none of that," Marbury said. "We don't have a strategy. In order to win games, you have to have a defensive strategy and an offensive strategy. We are discombobulated."

Coach John Calipari was immediately fired. Assistant coach Don Casey was named interim coach. He would take over until a new head coach could be found. The players quickly turned to Marbury for leadership. They asked him to shoulder the weight of their losing ways. The entire Nets franchise reached out for him. Was it too much to ask of a young, third-year player? "I've had the weight of New York City on my shoulders since I was a child. This ain't nothing," he said. "There was more pressure on me to make a foul shot to win the championship. That was pressure."

Marbury yelled at his teammates in practice. You want to be a winner, he said, you have to work like a winner. They listened. Marbury's impact was swift and clear. In New Jersey's very next game, Marbury's first home game in Nets uniform, the players hustled on defense, crashed into screens, pounded the boards, and executed on offense.

They beat the Dallas Mavericks before a vocal crowd at Continental Airlines Arena in a game that may have marked the turning point for the future. "I think the guys got tired of hearing me holler," said Marbury. "I guess they got annoyed with me and finally said, 'Let's just do it.'"

The Nets were 3–16, and the season was already lost, when Marbury joined them. But he managed to lift the spirit of the entire franchise in 1999. He scored plenty—32 points and 37 points in two victories over the Washington Wizards, 36 points in a win over the Orlando Magic, and 41 in a triumph over the Milwaukee Bucks. He showed his teammates that being a complete player also meant playing defense. He smothered Allen Iverson, the league's top scorer, into a woeful 2-for-17 shooting night in a victory over the 76ers. He raised the confidence of his teammates so high that suddenly they were running the strong Indiana Pacers off the floor in a 120–98 drubbing.

New Jersey's losing ways continued in the 1999–2000

season as the Nets stumbled through a 31–51 campaign. Marbury did all he could to help his team win, but it never seemed to be quite enough. In a game in early November, he scored 39 points and passed out 7 assists at home against the Indiana Pacers.

Although New Jersey has struggled recently, with players such as Marbury and Keith Van Horn, the Nets have a promising future.

The Nets lost by seven points. Ten days later, he scored a game-high 31 points and had 8 assists against the Charlotte Hornets. The Nets lost that game by four. Five days later, he scored 35 points and added 7 assists when the Nets played the Detroit Pistons. But the Nets lost by two. And so it went for Marbury and his team.

As the season entered the year 2000, the Nets did manage to win some big games. And no game was bigger for Marbury than the contest in February in Minneapolis against his former Timberwolves teammates. A national television audience watched Marbury celebrate his twenty-third birthday by scoring several clutch baskets down the stretch to lead his team to a narrow victory. Not only did the Nets win the game, 81–79, but Marbury scored nearly half his team's points, pouring in 39. What a birthday present!

Marbury finished the season leading the team in scoring (22.2 points per game) and assists (8.4 per game). But his team lost 20 more games than it won, and Marbury could never get used to losing. So in the off-season he worked harder than ever before. He watched tapes of games over and over again, rewinding the tape to analyze plays and the moves of players. He went to a local gym every night to shoot hundreds of baskets alone until midnight, doing all he could to get better.

Will the Nets be winners? Stephon Marbury intends to make it so with all his heart and soul. "We must be winners," he says. "That's why I work harder now than I did two years ago. Every minute I'm not working, someone else is. Right now, someone's lifting, someone's running, someone's shooting jump shots. That's why I can't stop."

Career Statistics

NBA

Year	Team	GP	FG%	REB	AST	STL	PTS	APG	PPG
1996–97	Minnesota	67	.408	184	522	67	1,057	7.8	15.8
1997–98	Minnesota	82	.415	230	704	104	1,450	8.6	17.7
1998–99	Minnesota New Jersey	49	.428	142	437	59	1,044	8.9	21.3
1999–2000	New Jersey	74	.432	240	622	112	1,640	8.4	22.2
Totals		272	.421	796	2,285	342	5,191	8.4	19.1

GP=Games Played   AST=Assists   APG=Assists Per Game
FG%=Field Goal Percentage   STL=Steals   PPG=Points Per Game
REB=Rebounds   PTS=Points

Where to Write Stephon Marbury:

Mr. Stephon Marbury
c/o New Jersey Nets
390 Murray Hill Parkway
East Rutherford, NJ 07073

On the Internet at:

http://www.nba.com/playerfile/stephon_marbury.html
http://www.nba.com/Nets

Index